Broker Price Opinions

The Complete Guide

By Jesse Brewer

Broker Price Opinions – The Complete Guide

LEGAL NOTICE

ISBN: 1440486069
EAN-13: 978-1440486067

Publisher: Createspace.com
Editor: ABCWriters.com

Contents

Introduction

In the past year, the economy has become increasingly difficult. Millions of Americans are losing their homes to foreclosure or they must short sell to avoid foreclosure. This creates a ripe new niche for the real estate agent who is not selling very many homes during these times of economic despair.

Each day, banks and other financial institutions are ordering thousands of Broker Price Opinions, which are like mini-appraisals. These institutions need up-to-date values on a property for one of the following reasons:

- The property will be sold after the foreclosure process
- A short sale will take place to avoid the foreclosure process
- The owner needs to refinance

This creates an opportunity for real estate agents who know how to take BPO orders and execute them. If you are doing BPO orders, besides making money on the order itself, you will open up other opportunities as well. The most obvious opportunity is to become a listing agent for the BPO subject property.

Often, payments on properties in pre-foreclosure are only a couple of months behind, and if you understand the process of short sales, then you can perhaps make some commissions for yourself by finding a buyer for the property.

In the current housing market, most real estate agents are making a mass exodus from the marketplace. By adding BPOs to your arsenal of revenue generating techniques, you cannot only survive in this troubled market, but you can also thrive. BPOs are a niche market with a growing need. Given the current downturn, REO listings and BPOs are definitely here to stay. You might as well get acquainted with them and generate some nice income in the process.

1 – What is a BPO?

BPO stands for Broker Price Opinion. A BPO is required when a broker, a real estate broker, or a real estate agent (also referred to herein as a "BPO agent") looks at a property and uses comparable sales, better known as "comps," to determine a realistic market value of the property. There are several factors that an agent/broker must consider when conducting these BPOs:

- Comparable properties must be similar in size, age, and amenities.
- Comparable properties must be within a certain radius of the subject property.
- Most lenders do not want comps to be REO properties; rather, they want consumer-sold properties.

- BPO agents must provide photos of the subject property as well as photos of comparable properties.
- Most lenders want three comparable SOLD properties and three comparable ACTIVE LISTING properties. Active listing properties are actively on the market for sale.

All of these factors will go to the lender for analysis and that lender will use the information to determine the true value of the property.

The BPO is a tool traditionally used by lenders foreclosing on a property—be it residential or commercial—to help determine the current market value of the property when deciding on a sale. In recent years, the use of the BPO has been expanded to accommodate other functions as well. Banks can order BPOs for various reasons:

- When a borrower wants to refinance their home, a bank can use a BPO to determine market value.

- When a borrower is attempting to get Primary Mortgage Insurance, better known as PMI, taken off their loan.
- When a short sale is being performed on a property, a BPO is ordered to determine market value.
- When an REO listing is sitting in inventory and the bank is getting ready to drop the price, they will order a BPO to determine current market value.

There are advantages to a bank using a BPO as opposed to a traditional appraisal on properties. The biggest factor is the cost associated with the BPO as opposed to the appraisal. Depending on the region of the country you live in, an appraisal on a residential property can cost roughly $300 to $500, while a BPO will only cost the bank $75 to $100. For a fraction of the cost the bank can gather the same information they need from an appraisal.

In many cases, the banks will order multiple BPOs on a property, especially in the case of a foreclosure. Because a BPO by title is an "opinion" of price by a broker, banks want to be sure that they get more than one opinion before making a decision about selling a property, issuing a new loan on a property, or taking a short sale payoff on a property.

The number of BPOs performed on a property may vary from region to region but it is usually somewhere in the 3-5 range depending on the market volatility and other factors such as declining markets and amount of other foreclosure, or REO properties on the market in that region.

2 – The Benefits of Doing BPOs

If you are a real estate licensee, this current real estate slowdown has probably adversely affected your income. BPOs can be a great way to generate additional revenue between real estate closings. For each BPO you complete, you can expect to earn roughly $40 to $60, and more when a BPO company puts a rush on the order. In these cases you can expect to earn roughly $100 to $150.

Most BPOs can be completed in less than thirty minutes, excluding the time required to take photos of the subject property. You can make best use of your time by processing multiple orders. I suggest taking the photos for all of your BPO orders at a certain time, and then inputting all the information later. This will increase your effectiveness by increasing your "hourly rate" for performing them.

Some agents in my local area have systemized their BPO business and have turned it into a six-figure income. In doing so, they have removed themselves from other real estate functions and have become strictly BPO professionals. Some of these BPO professionals do not take on REO listings; they just take new BPO orders and work from volume.

Another benefit associated with performing BPOs is that they can ultimately lead to REO listings (and the associated commissions) along with the possibility of picking up new clients as buyers of these REO/foreclosure properties. To prove your effectiveness, most companies require that you perform BPOs for some amount of time before they give you the listings. This can be a very lucrative niche if you can build yourself a solid reputation with the BPO companies and prove you capable for the task.

In order to build a reputation with the BPO companies, you need to keep a few things in mind. First of all BPO companies are looking for a quick turnaround of orders. In most instances you will get 48 to 72 hours to complete the BPO. Second, and arguably more important, BPO companies are concerned with the values you bring the property in at. This is not a case of bigger is better, so you should get out of the traditional mindset of finding the highest and best possible comps; rather, find realistic market comps. BPO companies want to know what a property will sell for. One problem occurs when a BPO agent brings the property in at an *inflated* value with the hope of getting the listing. But the BPO company is receiving multiple opinions, and if one opinion is out of line, then chances are that BPO agent will see fewer orders in the future. Just be honest and realistic about the properties, and you will be successful in the BPO industry.

Another often overlooked benefit is this: if you are an agent and also a real estate investor, then you can use BPOs as a lead generation source. A good percentage of the BPO orders are for homes going into foreclosure. If a BPO is being ordered, chances are the payments are just a few months behind, but not enough to take the property to the courthouse steps for auction. This is a good chance for a savvy investor to make a good deal on a possible short sale with the lender. When a homeowner is behind on their payments, they will often welcome solutions that will help them escape a foreclosure. These are valid leads and you can send them your letter and even possibly follow up with a home visit.

Just remember to always disclose your agency status when you become a possible buyer of these properties. If a short sale is not in order, you can always do a "subject to existing financing" deal, which is outside the scope of this text, or you can even attempt to find another investor in your client list who can step in and purchase the short sale. If you can consummate a deal, you can earn yourself a nice commission and possibly even make proceeds from the sale.

There are many positives to doing BPOs. If you are trying to earn extra income or if you are a savvy real estate investor with a real estate license there is something useful for you in the world of BPOs. Also remember: if you are an agent, to be sure to get any BPO activities cleared with your principal broker or with a person in your office who is designated to handle such matters.

3 – Signing Up to Receive BPOs

Once you've located the BPO companies, and you are at the registration step, things can get more complicated. A lot of BPO companies want their BPO agents to have at least two years experience as a licensee. I do know of several agents with less than two years who filled out the forms saying they do have the experience and they still got the BPO work.

Now we can consider some of the about other things you will need to register as a BPO agent. BPO companies will want you to complete a w-9, which most will have available on their website. You can also obtain your own blank form, fill it out, and fax it in. o. You will be working as an independent contractor, so be sure to file appropriately for taxes.

BPO companies will also want a photocopy of your real estate or appraiser's license. Some may even want a copy of your photo identification. I recommend scanning a copy of your real estate or appraiser's license into your computer along with a W-9 and photo identification. There are several hundred BPO companies out there, and you will want to sign up with as many as you can to start generating work. It will be a lot easier if you submit your application online or via email. Most BPO companies will give you the option and ability to do so, and this is much simpler than faxing and using US mail.

Other things you will need are your broker's tax identification number; however, some companies will pay you direct and only require your social security number. Be sure to check the local laws in your state as well as your broker's policy before taking payments directly from a company. You will also need to fill in the zip codes for the areas you are willing to take orders in. This is extremely important when setting up as a BPO agent because these companies are not familiar with your local geography, and if you don't enter the zip codes of the areas you will work in, then you will likely miss a lot of potential BPO orders.

After you have successfully signed up as a BPO agent, the orders will arrive in various ways depending on which company you have signed up with. The most popular way for BPO companies to send orders is via a broadcast method. A broadcast method is when the company emails the order out to five or so BPO agents and the first one to accept the order gets it. If you have a Blackberry® (from Verizon Wireless), there is a good chance you can be notified and accept the order via your Blackberry®. Some companies, Land America for example, uses software that will not interface with a Blackberry®. What that means is you have to accept the order on a computer. So you can see the email come in on your Blackberry® but you will need to get to your computer to accept it. Land America is a large BPO company, and they are usually one of the first to send you orders once you sign up.

BPO companies also email orders to a "queue box" on their website and then notify you via email that you have orders that need to be accepted. They give you four to eight hours to log onto their website and accept the orders in your queue. Countrywide Financial uses this method, and they are one of my favorite BPO companies.

Some companies do not notify you via email that you have orders at all. They expect you to periodically log onto their website and check your queue for orders in your area. They will make the order available to the BPO agents until someone accepts it.

To summarize, once you are set up properly to receive orders, you need to understand how each company puts out BPO orders and you will need to accommodate that method. After doing BPOs for a while, you will likely end up working for a few different companies that give you steady orders to fill. You will find a company that you work well with.

One factor in choosing the better BPO companies is the input form. Each one is different with respect to how long it takes to do an order and what particular information they require. In my opinion, the most important thing to consider is how quickly these companies pay you for your services. Some are quicker than others. I have found both good and bad paying companies.

4 – Equipment Needed

Not much equipment is needed to get started doing BPOs. You probably have most of it already; however, I'm going to describe the tools needed and why.

1) ***Automobile*** – More than likely you already own an automobile. If not you will need some method of transportation to and from the BPO properties.

2) ***Digital Camera*** – Any decent digital camera will do. Just be sure it has zoom capability and has memory disc capability. The camera I use cost me only $70. A big part of each BPO will be the photos of the subject properties. Thus, the zoom capability is important so you can take pictures from the street of small details like numbers on the house without trespassing on the property. Make sure to keep an

extra set of batteries as a backup.

3) *Navigation System* – A navigation system, or GPS, will help you find your properties. You will not have to print maps off the Internet or use an old fashioned map. You can get a decent GPS for less than $200. While not a necessity, a GPS will definitely make your BPO work much easier and more efficient.

4) *Personal Computer* – This is an important piece of equipment for interacting with BPO companies. If you are a licensed agent, you probably already own a computer. You can use it to input the BPO information online. All of your BPO business will be done via the Internet. A basic E-machine will work fine, and you can buy a good one for less than $500.

5) *Blackberry® Wireless Device* – Because most BPO orders are sent out in the broadcast format, in order to respond quickly, you will need to have constant access

to your email. Again, this is not a requirement; however, without it you will not be doing as many BPO orders. I've seen these Blackberrys® go on special sales (depending on the carrier you use) in the $135 range.

6) **Multiple Listing Service (MLS) access** – BPOs are impossible to complete without having the latest access to comparable sales and comparable listings.

7) **Internet Connection** – Any speed will do

8) **Real Estate License** - Standard

Once you have the above items, and once you have signed up and been cleared as a BPO agent, you can begin doing BPO work for those BPO companies you have signed up with.

5 – Filling Out the BPO Form

Gathering Information

Photos

Let's assume that you have accepted an order for a BPO and you now need to complete it.

The most common type of BPO is an exterior BPO. This is where you take photos of the outside of the property and do not go inside. Most BPO companies will want a photo of the front of the residence, one of the rear of the residence, one of the house numbers for address verification, one of the streetscape (this can be accomplished by taking a picture down the street from the home) and they will want a photo of what is across the street. Some BPO companies will vary slightly in their photo requirements, but generally this is what you'll be shooting.

You may have some problems getting all of the required photos, especially if the home is occupied and it's a foreclosure. Your safety is priority number one, and you should be aware that in some instances, people in the home know they are losing it and are not necessarily happy about it. They may consider you as a symbol of the bank or part of the institution taking their home. I've personally been chased and have had rocks and other inanimate objects thrown at me. So you need to be prepared for this and cautious at all times. If your broker allows it, and your state laws permit it, I'd suggest looking into a concealed carry permit or some form of self-defense to protect yourself.

Always be mindful of the law. Do not trespass to photograph the rear of the residence. In 95% of the BPOs I have done, I was not able to get a rear photo. Instead, I stand to the side of the home and take a picture of the side, showing the depth of the house. In the comments section of the BPO form, I note that the rear of the property was inaccessible. Another problem photo may be the address verification photo. Sometimes you get lucky and the numbers are on the mailbox; however, there will be several instances in which this is not the case. This is where a digital camera with zoom capabilities will help you out because you can zoom into the front of the home. When there are no address numbers on the house or mailbox, I take a picture of the street sign and put in the comments section of the BPO form that there were no visible numbers and submit the photo of the street sign instead.

See Appendix for sample BPO photos.

Filling in the BPO form

So now you have your photo. You have downloaded them into your personal computer, and you are ready to fill in the BPO form. The particulars of this will vary with each BPO company;

however, most of the information needed is the same. Your form will be broken down into sections. Below, I discuss some the most common sections and tell you what the BPO company is looking for. Also, I've included a sample BPO form that you can turn to as a reference guide.

Subject property information

This section is near the top of the form and you will enter basic information on the subject property and about yourself. Here you will be required to fill in the following types of information about the subject property:

- *Address* – The physical address of the property.
- *Age* – How old the property is. This can be found in the MLS or tax records.
- *Square footage* – The amount of living space.
- *Bed and bath count* – How many bed and baths are in the house.
- *Style of house* – Ranch, two-story, bi-level or tri-level etc.

- *Previous sale history* – Check the MLS to see last sale date and if it was listed and never sold.
- *Your opinion of condition of the property* – Here they want to know what the exterior looks like: excellent, fair, or poor.
- *Your opinion of neighborhood quality* – Here they are asking if you think there is a lot of pride in ownership in the neighborhood or if it is run down and not cared for. This is purely a judgment on your part.
- *Your information* – They will also want information about you: how far your office is from the subject property, the date you inspected the property, your experience etc.

The next sections will be your comparable properties section. All the BPO companies I've done work for have a similar comps section. They will want three *sold comparable* properties and three *active listings*. The information they are looking for on the sold comps will be:

- The physical address of the property
- The age of the property
- The square footage of the property
- How many bedrooms and bathrooms there are
- Distance the comp is from the subject property
- The sold date of the property
- How many days on the market the property was
- The original listing price
- The sales price of the property
- The style of home (i.e. bi-level, tri-level two-story or ranch etc).

Some of the companies will want a photo of the comp as well. I always take this photo out of the Multiple Listing Service on the computer and submit that with the BPO.

When choosing your comp properties, be certain they are actual comparable properties. Use properties that are similar in age, size and style. BPO companies will have quality control mechanisms in place and will fail it if you do not use comparable properties. Some of these companies will have it automatically built in and will not let you submit it unless the parameters are met. Each company's parameters will be different so you will have to learn your companies and what they are looking for as you do more BPO orders.

Your BPO order will then require listing comps. Generally BPO companies want the same information here as with the sold comps with one exception: instead of having a sold date you will put a *listing date* in a field as well as *days on market* field. You will also need to note the *original list* price as well as the *current list* price.

The next fields of information required will be your opinion of value. This is based on the comparable sales data.

You will include your opinion of what the property will sell for in a *quick sale*—generally thirty days or less is a quick sale. As a rule of thumb, the number you put here should be within 20% of the value of the home, or it will fail quality control.

They will also ask you any other information about the subject property they need to know, and there will be a space for you to upload all your photos of the property. After this is complete, you will submit the BPO and you are finished, assuming it passes quality control and you don't get it back for corrections.

Making corrections

If you are doing a BPO for a company without automatic quality control, you may get it back for corrections. These corrections can be things like:

- Comparable properties not close enough in age.
- Comparable properties not close enough in size.

- The subject value is not within a certain percentage of the comparable properties (generally they are looking for twenty percent but this will vary from company to company).

If you get any of these, you need to correct the problem and resubmit as soon as you can for several reasons. First, you will not get paid for the BPO unless it meets their standards. Second, you will not get any more BPO orders until this one is corrected. Lastly, you want to minimize the overall required corrections because BPO companies track your performance and rate you based on the number of corrections, your accuracy in values, and your timeliness in getting the job done.

6 – Frequently Asked Questions

Here are some common questions related to the BPO process. Some are related to the agent directly; others to the banks or the BPO process.

How much money can I make doing BPOs?

Generally, as a new agent doing exterior BPOs, you can expect to earn anywhere from $40 to $60 per order. As a new BPO agent it is doubtful you will get a lot of orders; however, after a short period of time, you can find yourself doing twenty to thirty orders per month, or more.

How much money does it take me to get started doing BPOs?

Most of the start up expense is usually money you have already spent as a real estate agent. You need to be a licensed realtor or appraiser. You will need a digital camera and a vehicle (which are things you more than likely already have). One thing you may not have, which I highly recommend, is a navigation system for your vehicle (you can purchase one for less than $200). If you are not a member of the multiple listing service, you need to become one. The only other start up costs may be related to the expense associated the searching the Internet and buying a BPO list of companies if you don't already own one.

What licenses do I need to do BPOs?
You need to be either a licensed real estate agent or a licensed appraiser. If you are an appraiser, you likely will not be doing BPOs because you can do the same amount of work for a bank and make four times the money than you would doing BPOs. Some formal BPO training does exist on the Internet. It is not required, and I'm not sure if the lenders even care if you have it or not; however, it may assist you in getting started, and may also expose you to BPO companies these training programs cater to.

Why is it difficult so find BPO companies to work for?

If you are a new BPO agent, you might feel like you are trying to join a secret society! In a round about way you are. Because of the broadcast style these companies use to find agents to fill their orders, many of your fellow local agents are reluctant to give you information on where to sign up. To do so would be, in essence, taking orders from themselves. Not to worry: using the Internet, you can get the names of BPO companies, Try visiting real estate agent forums. The BPO companies do not advertise for agents because they do not need to. Plenty of agents are searching them out. Serious BPO agents can purchase a current list online, or they can utilize the list included with this eBook.

Is it true I can get REO listings from doing BPOs?

It depends. I know of agents who have done BPOs for years and have never gotten an REO listing; on the other hand, I know of agents who have done BPOs for a short time and began getting listings right away. BPO companies keep track of your performance before proactively giving you listings, but I do not know the formula they use to determine when they will start doing this. This will vary from company to company and from asset manager to asset manger within the BPO company. Once you start getting listings from a particular asset manager, be sure to cultivate the relationship as you will likely put yourself in a position for more listings in the future.

How many different types of BPOs are there?

There are many. The most common one that you, as a residential real estate agent, will be dealing with is the *drive-by exterior*. This is where you drive by the property, take your photos, and enter the information into your computer. Another type of BPO that is frequent but not quite as common as the drive by is the *interior inspection*. This is more in depth. You will enter the subject property and take photos of all the rooms and note the condition of each room. Here you will make more money for your time because there is more work involved. Lastly, you may see a *desktop BPO*. These do not require you to leave the office; rather, you merely check the MLS and tax records for comps and enter the required information to complete the BPO. Desktop BPOs do not pay quite as well and generally they can be completed in less than fifteen minutes.

Who am I actually working for when doing these BPOs?

Technically you are working for your real estate brokerage as an independent contractor. Your client is often an asset management company that has been contracted by a bank or lending institution to liquidate its real estate inventory, so the bank or lending institution is a client of the asset management company. This asset management company is in charge of collecting the information for the bank and charges a minimal fee. The bank or lending institution may have a couple different asset management companies performing BPOs and the management companies may be competing for the listings themselves. In some cases, if you are signed up with multiple companies, you may get the same subject property by more than one company to perform a BPO on. Some companies have policies preventing you from doing the work; however, this is an honor system, and it is your responsibility to notify them if you have previously done a BPO on the subject property or not.

How long does it take for me to get paid once I complete the BPO?

This will depend on the company you are working for. Some companies pay you in a timely manner; others do not. A good place to discover what companies are the best is www.agentsonline.net. It is a good forum for realtors who work in the BPO world. You can also sign up for BPO agents to see you, and you may get orders that way. I recommend visiting this site often if you are going to work in the BPO sector of real estate.

Why BPOs instead of appraisals?

Bottom line: MONEY. The bank will have multiple BPOs performed on a property for various reasons. They feel that a licensed agent can provide the same information as an appraiser can, and at a *fraction of the cost*. A full appraisal is similar to an interior BPO. In my opinion, the banks contradict themselves: when *they* are spending the money, they allow agents to do inexpensive BPOs; when *the consumer* is spending the money, they want a licensed appraiser.

As a newer agent, would you recommend BPOs as a part of my business?

Absolutely yes! This can be a great way to generate cash and leads as well as helping you become more familiar with the neighborhoods in your locale.

Do I need a bunch of equipment to do a BPO?

No. You need a digital camera, computer, and a vehicle.

How much experience do I need to get started?

Most BPO companies require a minimum of two years experience as a licensed agent or appraiser.

Notes on Filling out the application:
I never condone falsifying any documentation or records; however, several people in the industry I've spoken with have indicated that most BPO companies do not verify your years of experience. Newly licensed agents have been known to sign up to be BPO agents and be successful at getting the BPO work and not meet the minimum requirements.

Who can complete BPOs

Not just any person can complete BPOs. Although the requirements are not stringent, certain licenses must be obtained before doing BPOs. You must either be a licensed realtor or appraiser, and many BPO companies require that you have held these licenses for a minimum of two years.

Note however that just being licensed does not mean you can do BPOs anywhere. You can only perform BPOs in the states in which you are licensed. If you live in an area where your local economy crosses over state lines, then you will need a license in both of these states in order to perform BPOs. For example I live in an region where local economies in both Ohio and Kentucky interchange. I have a real estate license in both states, so I can perform BPOs in both locales.

BPOs are designed to be extra income or side revenue. So if you're getting one of the above licenses for the sole purposes of BPOs, chances are you will not make enough money for it to be worth your time and investment. If you are already one of the above professionals and you are looking for extra income, especially in this slow market, then BPOs may be just the niche you are looking for.

7 – Increasing Your BPO Business

You might be asking yourself how you can increase your BPO business. This is a question I consistently get from new BPO agents. I can tell you there is no 100% correct answer. There are ways to pick up orders and there are also pitfalls that cause you to lose orders once you start increasing your BPO business.

Once you start doing BPO orders, the BPO companies want to see how good you are before they give you more orders. You need to be sure that you complete your orders on time—and early is always preferred. Take your time and make sure to submit it without errors. If you consistently do this, you will increase your rating system with that company and more orders will follow as your rating increases. Most BPO companies look at the following performance criteria: 1) completing the order on time, 2) getting the order submitted with no required corrections, and 3) in the event corrections are needed, how fast you get them completed.

If a company calls you personally to accept an order, be sure to do everything in your power to accept it for them. This will give you an opportunity to open a personal dialogue with an individual who is in charge of sending BPO orders out for that company. You can help them with difficult or rush orders. You will become someone they can count on, and if you do this enough times, it will lead you into more orders and quite possibly into the REO listings themselves.

Also be sure to expand the territory you are willing to cover. During the sign-up phase with a new company, you will have an opportunity to input either zip codes or counties for your area of coverage. You might consider putting in a larger area to ensure you start getting orders. The first few orders you get may be off the beaten path; however, once you improve your rating, you will get more orders in the areas you cover. At that point you can revise the territory sections you have made.

You can also use technology to create more work for yourself. If you have a partner or an assistant who is near a computer, you can have them constantly checking the websites and watching your email to grab orders when they first hit. A Blackberry® can help you here.

Also have your assistant check the BPO companies that do not broadcast orders and list them on there site instead. Some agents do only BPOs and have team members with the sole responsibility of accepting orders. You might offer someone in your office a few dollars for every order they successfully accept and bring in for you.

When you just starting out though the two biggest things to remember are register with as many companies as you can and to make your territory as large as you are comfortable closing.

This is sort of the law of large numbers in the BPO industry. As time goes on and you complete more orders you will develop the contacts and relationships necessary to make some great extra cash at this.

8 – Sample BPO Form

Every BPO company will have a different form, but most of them are similar with respect to the information they ask for. Following is a sample BPO form to give you an idea of what they look like and the information necessary to complete the process.

Broker Price Opinion

PROPERTY ADDRESS:

REO #:			**BORROWER:**		

Most Recent Listing History	From		To		Listed at $

I.   GENERAL MARKET CONDITIONS

Current market condition.	☐ Depressed	☐ Slow	☐ Stable	☐ Improving	☐ Excellent

II.   SUBJECT MARKETABILITY

Normal marketing time in the area is:		days.				
Marketability of subject property is	☐ excellent	☐ good	☐ fair	☐ poor.		
Unit Type:	☐ House	☐ Condo	☐ Townhouse	☐ Multi-family (#. of units)		☐ Modular

III.   COMPETITIVE ACTIVE LISTINGS

ITEM	SUBJECT			COMPARABLE NO. 1			COMPARABLE NO. 2			COMPARABLE NO. 3		
Address												
Proximity to ¦ ubj.												
Current Price :												
List Date /DOM												
Lot Size												
Room Count	Total	Bdrms	Baths	Total	Bdrms	Baths	Total	Bdrms	Baths	Total	Bdrms	Baths
Room Count												
Gross Living Area		sq. Ft.			sq. Ft.			sq. Ft.			sq. Ft.	

COMMENTS Please describe the condition of the comparables
COMP #1:
COMP #2:
COMP #3:

IV.   COMPETITIVE CLOSED SALES

ITEM	SUBJECT			COMPARABLE NO. 1			COMPARABLE NO. 2			COMPARABLE NO. 3		
Address												
Proximity to ¦ ubj.												
Sales Price $												
Date of Sale / DOM												
Lot Size												
Room Count	Total	Bdrms	Baths	Total	Bdrms	Baths	Total	Bdrms	Baths	Total	Bdrms	Baths
Room Count												
Gross Living Area		sq. Ft.			sq. Ft.			sq. Ft.			sq. Ft.	

COMMENTS Please describe the condition of the comparables.
COMP #1:
COMP #2:
COMP #3:

V.   ESTIMATED CLOSING COSTS / REPAIRS NOTED

Gross Estimated Closing Costs	
Gross Amount of Repairs Needed	
List of Repairs (if necessary)	

List of Repairs (if necessary) Continued....	

VI.   THE MARKET VALUE must fall within the indicated value of the sales used above.

THE VALUE FOR THE SUBJECT PROPERTY BASED ON 120 DAYS LIST TO CONTRACT IS:

	Market Value	Suggested List Price	Available Financing	Broker Recommends Marketing Either
As Is	$	$	Conv ☐ FHA/VA ☐ Other ☐	As Is ☐ OR
Complete Repairs	$	$	Estimate of Repairs: $	Repairs ☐

COMMENTS including specific positive on this property and special concerns, if any, like apparent structural issues, encroachments, easements, water rights, propane, hazardous waste, flood zone, etc.) Attach addendum if additional space is needed.

....

....

....

....

_____   _____
Agent's Signature   Date

9 – Nationwide List of BPO Companies

Many readers probably flipped to this section of the book first. This may even be the sole reason you bought this book. All kidding aside here is a list of companies I've complied over the years.

Website	Phone Number
www.rrreview.com	904-722-7012
www.safeguardproperties.com	800-852-8306
www.mgic.com	800-424-6442
www.protk.com	800-886-4949
www.remusa.com	888-736-7945
www.nascopgh.com	866-357-5660
www.sourceoneservices.com	801-303-2400
www.advantagevaluation.com	858-866-0808
www.appraisalbank.org	214-943-9990
www.workflow.fasinc.com	949-862-1418
www.premierebpo.com	973-316-9339
www.mdwebbinc.com	949-474-0599
www.islandadvantagerealty.com	800-368-3808

Website	Phone Number
www.csappraisal.net	877-352-4650
www.provalu.com	978-283-2873
singlesourceproperty.com	866-620-7577
www.lendersreo.com	303-979-6350
bpodirect.com	N/A
www.reoworld.com	949-720-7009
www.assetval.com	970-245-735
ladsvalues.landam.com/index.html	949-474-4505
cwfieldservices.com/valuations.asp	888-554-4690
www.imortgageservices.com	412-220-7330
www.emortgagelogic.com/index.html	817-581-2900
www.clearcapital.com	N/A
www.iasreo.com	303-770-1976
www.iasreo.com	303-770-1976
www.evaluateusa.com	972-485-4477
www.gobpo.com	818-226-1331
www.cartelbpo.com	303-420-6900
www.quickbpo.com	800-776-1815
www.BPOsonline.com	432-684-9802
brokerpriceopinion.com	303-991-9919
www.emcmortgagecorp.com	N/A
www.evalonline.com	904-425-1300
www.nationwideBPOs.com	512-291-2331
www.farvv.com	877-771-7711
www.homesteps.com	N/A
www.reoagents.net	N/A
www.evalue8america.com	N/A
www.mainstreetval.com	801-464-4093

When I first starting doing BPOs, I registered with all the above companies. With the changing market, I cannot warrant that this list will be current at the time you read this book, but this will be a good starting place for you to get established doing BPO orders. I recommend that you also search the Internet for other available lists.

My favorite of these sites is Countrywide, located at:

www.cwfieldservices.com

Countrywide does not use the broadcast method. Instead, they email you the orders and give you four to eight hours to accept them. For me, turnaround times were always five days (except on rush orders) and turnaround time on pay was very prompt.

Good luck!

Appendix

Sample Photos

Subject photo – exterior

Subject photo – rear

Subject photo – rear alternative shot. When you can't trespass, this shot is what you need.

Subject address verification photo. This is where you need the numbers of the subject property's address.

Subject photo – Across the street from the subject. BPO companies want this to see what types of housing the subject sits near, and this will also verify to the bank that you actually went to the property to obtain the photographs. Remember, there likely be more than one BPO performed on the property.

Streetscape photo from in front of the subject. This is taken to indicate if the subject is on a busy street or a residential-type street. From this photo, it appears that the subject is on a cul-de-sac street.

Made in the USA
Lexington, KY
09 March 2010